ENIGMAS *of* HISTORY

THE SECRETS OF
THE PHARAOHS

WORLD
BOOK

a Scott Fetzer company
Chicago
www.worldbook.com

World Book edition of "Enigmas de la historia" by Editorial Sol 90.

Enigmas de la historia
Los secretos de los faraones

This edition licensed from Editorial Sol 90 S.L.
Copyright 2013 Editorial Sol S.L. All rights reserved.

English-language revised edition copyright 2014
World Book, Inc.
Enigmas of History
The Secrets of the Pharaohs

World Book, Inc.
233 North Michigan Avenue
Suite 2000
Chicago, Illinois, 60601 U.S.A.

For information about other World Book publications,
visit our website at **www.worldbook.com** or call
1-800-967-5325.

Library of Congress Cataloging-in-Publication Data

Secretos de los faraones. English.
   The secrets of the pharaohs. -- English-language revised
edition.
   pages cm. -- (Enigmas of history)
   Orignially published as: Secretos de los faraones, by
Editorial Sol S.L., c2013.
   Includes bibliographical references and index.
   Summary: "An exploration of the questions and
mysteries surrounding the pharaohs of Egypt. Features
include a map, fact boxes, biographies of famous experts
on ancient Egypt, places to see and visit, a glossary,
further readings, and index"-- Provided by publisher.
   ISBN 978-0-7166-2666-4
   1. Pharaohs--Juvenile literature. 2. Egypt--Kings and
rulers--Juvenile literature. I. World Book, Inc. II. Title.
DT61.S42313 2014
932'.01--dc23
                              2014011197

Set ISBN: 978-0-7166-2660-2

Printed in the U.S.A. and assembled in Mexico.
1st printing June 2014

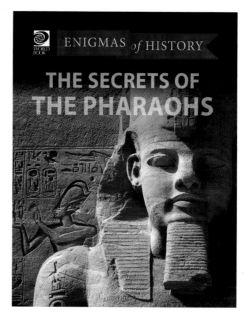

A huge statue of the powerful pharaoh Ramses II
dominates the temple complex of Abu Simbel, near
Aswan. The temple was built from around 1260
to 1240 B.C., in what was then Nubia, to impress
Egypt's neighbors to the south. In the 1960's, this
entire complex was taken apart, relocated to higher
ground, and reassembled after the Aswan Dam
raised the level of the Nile River and threatened to
leave the original site under water.

© F1online/Alamy images

Staff

Contents

6   Questions From the Beginnings of History

8   The Land of the Nile

16   The Egypt of the Pharaohs

18   Symbols of Power

20   Why Were Pharaohs Mummified?

22   Who Built the First Pyramid?

24   Which Pharaoh Built the Greatest of the Pyramids?

26   The Great Sphinx of Giza

28   Did They Marry Their Sisters?

30   Akhenaten and Nefertiti

34   Decline and Recovery

36   Who Were the Black Pharaohs?

38   Who Was Cleopatra?

40   Identification of Mummies

42   Places to See and Visit

44   Glossary

45   For Further Information

46   Index

48   Acknowledgments

Questions From the Beginnings of History

Egypt is a land of many mysteries, and tales of the treasures and secrets of the pharaohs have fascinated people since the time of the ancient Greeks and Romans. Ancient Egypt's forgotten writing, great age, monumental ruins, buried treasure, secret religious beliefs, and magnificent gold and jewels all make for a gripping subject.

Archaeology (the scientific study of the remains of past human cultures) and *genetics* (the scientific study of heredity, the passing on of characteristics of living organisms from one generation to the next) have combined to give us a somewhat clearer picture of who the ancient Egyptians were and where they came from, but many unknowns remain. Why did the ancestors of the Egyptians first settle in Egypt, and how were they able to create such a long-lasting and successful *civilization* (society or culture that has complex

social, political, and economic institutions) in the middle of a barren desert?

The oldest wonder of the ancient world is the Great Pyramid at Giza. What ruler created this amazing tomb? We know his name was Khufu (KOO foo) and that he lived around 2550 B.C., but his tomb was robbed in ancient times, and we know very little else about him. Near the pyramid at Giza is the great monument known as the Sphinx. How this great art was created and its purpose are both unknown.

The stories of the pharaohs can be mysterious. For example, the history of Hatshepsut (hat SHEHP soot—ruled from about 1473-1458 B.C.) is unusual. Other women ruled as pharaohs; she was actually the fourth to do so. But she was the only woman to be depicted in art as a man, with a false beard and the headcloth of a pharaoh. What made her choose such a depiction of herself? Hatshepsut originally ruled in place of Thutmose (thoot MOH suh) III (about 1479-1425 B.C.), a son of her late husband too young to rule in his own right. Why was Hatshepsut removed from many of the records of pharaohs and other histories some 20 years after her death? Who was responsible for the removals? Scientists found her mummy in 2007 and were able to determine that she likely died of bone cancer, but they do not know who tried to erase her from memory.

The fates of the pharaoh considered to be a *heretic* (a person holding beliefs that are different from accepted beliefs), Akhenaten (AH kuh NAH tehn—ruled from about 1353 to 1336 B.C.) and his beautiful wife Nefertiti (NEHF uhr TEE tee) have long intrigued people. New theories and evidence have changed our ideas about the end of the Amarna Age (the age in the mid-1300's B.C. when Akhenaten ruled) and what happened to the members of the royal family from that time. But questions remain. What were the reasons that Amenhotep IV changed his name to Akhenaten? Why did he change the traditional worship of many gods to a single deity, the Aten (AH tuhn)? Did the unusual art style depicting him during his reign reflect some sort of physical illness suffered by the pharaoh? Had marriage between close family members over generations created a genetic disease in Akhenaten?

Scientists began analyzing *DNA* (chain-like molecules found in every living cell on earth that direct the formation, growth, and reproduction of cells and organisms) on the royal mummies in the Cairo Museum. This work revealed new evidence as to what types of illnesses were found in the "boy king" pharaoh, Tutankhamun. It also allowed scientists to learn about Tutankhamun's father, Akhenaten, and the ancestors of these pharaohs. Tutankhamun, born to Akhenaten and his sister, was originally named Tutankhaten, meaning *the living image of Aten.* Why, during his reign, did he change his name and change Egypt back to the old religion practiced before his father's time?

These are just some of the many mysteries that new scientific research is helping us to understand. The combined work of dedicated archaeologists in the field, scientists in the laboratory, and historians in ancient libraries has given us new insight into some of the secrets of the pharaohs. Who knows what else remains to be discovered?

The Land of the Nile

More than 4,000 years of unequaled stability made Egypt into a great power of the ancient world and a model for future kingdoms. There are thousands of enigmas yet to be resolved about Egypt's rulers, the pharaohs, because of this lengthy history.

E gypt is a gift from the Nile. This was the view of the Greek historian and traveler Herodotus (484?-425? B.C.), author of the monumental *Histories*, the first notable historical record in the ancient world. To a practical man like Herodotus, Egypt was merely "the country that the Nile watered with its floods and the Egyptians were those who live downstream from the city of Elephantine and drink water from that river." Herodotus could not have imagined how this brief, matter-of-fact description would open the doors to a land full of marvels to be discovered by future generations.

From the first waterfall to the south of Elephantine, through the lands of Nubia (an ancient African region that covered part of what is now Sudan), to the river's mouth at the Mediterranean Sea, the waters of the River Nile brought life to an extraordinary and long-lived civilization.

Before the time of the pharaohs, a wave of *nomads* (people who move from place to place as a way of obtaining food) from North Africa had settled down to farm and raise livestock on the riverbanks and the nearby *oases* (fertile areas in a desert where underground water comes close enough to the surface for wells). These somewhat dark times, known as Dynasty Zero (5550-3100 B.C.) and led by the Horus kings, ended about 2950 B.C., at the Early Dynastic Period.

FIRST WRITING

In 1997, at the tomb of Umm el-Qaab, near the ancient city of Abydos, German archaeologist Gunter Dreyer found clay vessels and tablets with *inscriptions* (carved letters and symbols) that dated to around 3200 B.C., just before the Early Dynastic Period. These inscriptions may be proof of the most ancient writing system known, even older than *cuneiform* (kyoo NEE uh fawrm—an ancient writing system that used wedge-shaped letters) of Mesopotamia (a region that included the area that is now Iraq, eastern Syria, and southeastern Turkey). This early writing was found in the tomb of Scorpion I (3200 B.C.), who is believed to have been the first king of Upper Egypt (see map on page 16). Ceramic jars containing the remains of what seems to have been wine were also found in this king's tomb.

FIRST PHARAOH

During the time known as the Early Dynastic Period (2950-2650 B.C.), the country of the Two Lands, Lower Egypt to the north and Upper Egypt to the south, were united under the first pharaoh.

Scholars are not certain as to who this first pharaoh was. The discovery of a clay tablet and a limestone hammer at Hierakonpolis in 1897 led to Narmer, King of Upper Egypt, being credited as the first. Some Egyptologists have suggested Aha, Narmer's child and successor, as a candidate for the first pharaoh. Menes is also credited as the first ruler of a unified Egypt, from about 2950 B.C. This does not really answer who was first. Pharaohs had several names, and *Egyptologists* (scientists who study ancient Egypt) are not agreed upon whether Menes was Narmer,

RAMSES II
Monumental sculptures of the powerful Pharaoh Ramses II at the entrance to the rock-carved temple at Abu Simbel

Aha, or another person as yet unknown to scholars.

FIRST STEP PYRAMID

In the Old Kingdom (about 2650-2150 B.C.) that followed the Early Dynastic Period, Zoser, who reigned in the 2600's B.C., ordered the first step pyramid to be built at Saqqara, the biggest *necropolis* (burial ground) in Memphis (see pages 22-23). The beginning of the next *dynasty* (period ruled by a new family) featured the perfect architecture of Snefru (about 2575-2550 B.C.), who built several pyramids in Meidum and Dahshur. (All dates given for pharaohs are for the years in which they ruled.) The best known of these are the Rhomboid Pyramid (a *rhomboid* is a figure with two parallel sides of equal length with the other two sides of a different, but also equal, length) and the North Pyramid (the second largest in Egypt).

Snefru's successor, Khufu—in Greek, Cheops—ruled for 23 years, approximately the same amount of time that it took to build the Great Pyramid at Giza (see pages 24-25). The largest of the Egyptian pyramids, it is made up of about 2.3 million limestone blocks. The other two pyramids of Giza, somewhat less grand, were built during the reign of Khafre—Chephren in Greek (2520-2495 B.C.)—and Menkaure—Mykerinos in Greek (2490-2470 B.C.). Next to the pyramid of Khafre, a gigantic sculpture of the Great Sphinx was carved. A sphinx is a creature from *myth* (a story of unknown origin, often one that attempts to account for events in nature or historical events from long ago). The Great Sphinx is a figure with the body of a lion and a human head. Historians believe that Khafre probably had the monument built.

Pyramid fever, evident in Abusir and Saqqara, lessened as the Old Kingdom progressed. The Pyramid Texts—inscriptions on the walls of the *antechamber* (a small room leading to a larger one) and the burial chamber first appeared in the Pyramid of Unas (2355-2325 B.C.). These texts describe *rituals* (religious ceremonies), *legends* (stories from the past), and *incantations* (words spoken or chanted as a magic charm or to cast a magic spell) to help the pharaoh after death in his travels through the afterlife.

The end of the Old Kingdom, around 2150 B.C., was marked by a period when there were more than 25 rulers in 50 years. This confused succession of rulers ushered in the First Intermediate Period (from about 2125-1975 B.C.) and led to the division of the country between two kingdoms, Herakleopolis in the north and Thebes in the south.

HORSES AND CHARIOTS

Around 1975 B.C., Pharaoh Mentuhotep from the Eleventh Dynasty of Thebes contributed to the fall of the Tenth Dynasty of Herakleopolis. Mentuhotep unified the Two Lands. His reign began the period known as Middle Kingdom (about 1975-1640 B.C.), and he turned Thebes into the new capital. He erected his burial temple at Deir el-Bahri (where Hatshepsut built her temple).

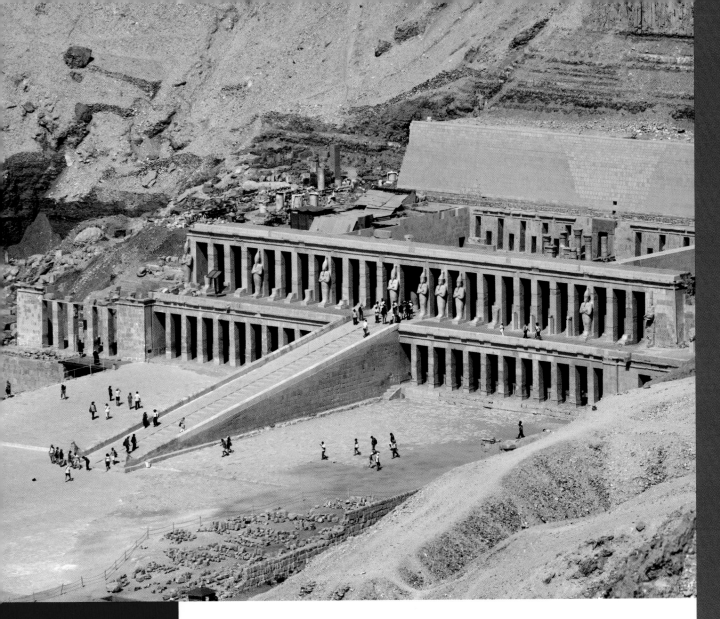

TIERED PYRAMID

The step pyramid (above left) was built by Pharaoh Zoser. It is the oldest stone monument in the world.

TEMPLE OF HATSHEPSUT

Located in the valley of Deir el-Bahri, the Temple of Hatshepsut is thought to have been designed by the architect Senenmut. Some Egyptologists believe he may have been the father of Pharaoh Hatshepsut's daughter Neferure.

It was a golden age during which there was internal peace and prosperity. There were, however, military campaigns against Libya, Canaan (later Palestine), and Nubia, undertaken to expand Egypt's borders, obtain minerals—particularly gold—and control trade routes. Senusret (she NOOS reht) I, the second pharaoh of the Twelfth Dynasty, who ruled from about 1918 to 1875 B.C., was responsible for the construction of the white chapel at Karnak, which is famous for its *reliefs* (carvings). Senusret also raised two red granite *obelisks* (OB uh lihskz)—great, upright, four-sided stone pillars. One of these obelisks—at Heliopolis—is still standing. It is the oldest of the great pillars preserved in Egypt.

The end of the Middle Kingdom in ancient Egypt is marked by the invasion of the Hyksos, immigrants from the land of Canaan to the east. Their kings established their capital at Avaris, at the Nile *delta* (a low plain composed of sediments deposited at the mouth of a river). From Avaris they governed Lower and Middle Egypt. The Hyksos introduced the horse, war chariots, and bronze *smelt-ing* (obtaining metal from ore by melting it) to Egypt.

THE NEW KINGDOM'S SPLENDOR

Ahmose (AH mohs) I became the first king of the Eighteenth Dynasty, in about 1539 B.C. This was the beginning of ancient Egypt's third and greatest period, which historians now call the New Kingdom. Ahmose I threw out the Hyksos and again established the capital of the Two Lands at Thebes. Scholars believe that the pyramid he ordered built in Abydos may have been the last one from the time of Ancient Egypt.

With Pharaoh Thutmose I (about 1493-? B.C.), the third king of the Eighteenth Dynasty, the borders of the country extended to the third waterfall in Nubia and the banks of the Euphrates in Mesopotamia. This monarch ordered that the Temple of Karnak, located to the north of Thebes and dedicated to the main deity Amun-Re, be enlarged. He also decided to build his tomb in the Valley of the Kings, near the desert hills west of Thebes. His was the first tomb of the New Kingdom in that valley. From then on, the traditional pyramid burial complex, which was also the object of plundering by grave robbers, was replaced by the *hypogeum* (an underground burial chamber) carved into a mountainside. His grandson, Thutmose III, was co-regent with the woman pharaoh, Hatshepsut, when he was young.

In the shadow of Hatshepsut, Thutmose III learned the role of pharaoh, which he was able to exercise with the spirit of a conqueror when he became 21 years old. The military conquests of this ruler, described as the "Egyptian Napoleon," seemed unlimited. His regime of conquest made him, as the sole king of the Two Lands, into the principal power of the Near East. Nubia (to the fourth waterfall of the Nile), the Near East, parts of North Africa, and the Phoenician coast were all within the borders of his kingdom.

Thutmose III also took on large architectural projects. In addition to a large number of temples and monuments, the festival hall and the red chapel at Karnak were built at his request.

Christiane Desroches-Noblecourt
(1913-2011)

Christiane Desroches-Noblecourt was a French Egyptologist with the Egyptian Antiquities Department of the Louvre Museum. She was the first woman to lead an excavation in Egypt. She dedicated her life to studying and protecting the pharaonic heritage, and especially to saving the temples of Abu Simbel and other Egyptian monuments in Nubia from flooding by the Aswan Dam project. She was the author of numerous works on Ancient Egypt, the reign of Ramses II, and the role of women in the time of the pharaohs.

COMMITTED. Desroches-Noblecourt gained international acclaim for her resolute campaign to protect the temples of Abu Simbel.

Nicholas Reeves
(1956-)

With a Ph.D. from Britain's Durham University, this Egyptologist has served as *curator* (overseer) of the departments of Egyptian Art at the British Museum, the New York Metropolitan Museum of Art, and private collections. He is known for his research in the Valley of Kings. In the year 2000, along with his colleague Geoffrey T. Martin, Reeves discovered an unexplored underground chamber while trying to find the tombs of the queens of the Seventeenth Dynasty. This was chamber KV63, a mummification room which contained coffins and jars, but no mummy.

VALLEY OF THE KINGS. Reeves maintains that the tombs of the queens of the Seventeenth Dynasty (never found) would be beside those of their husbands.

> *"As scientists, we must have an open mind, but our ideas about the past have to be based on archaeological evidence."* Z. H.

Zahi Hawass (1947-)

In recent decades, Hawass has been among the Egyptologists who have unraveled the greatest number of mysteries regarding ancient Egypt. The discovery of new passages in the Great Pyramid are among his findings. In 2005, he oversaw the *computed tomography* (CT, an advanced type of Xray) of the mummy of Tutankhamun, which allowed scientists to learn more about the possible causes of his early death. Hawass has focused on identifying the mummies in the Valley of the Kings, using new medical technologies. Thanks to his work, the mummies of queens Hatshepsut and Tiye (the wife of Amenhotep III and the mother of Pharaoh Akhenaten) were identified.

CONTROVERSIAL. Political controversy has surrounded Hawass for a number of years. In 2011, he was removed from his position as Egypt's Minister of Antiquities.

Mark Lehner (1950-)

This American archaeologist and Egyptologist is the foremost expert on the plateau of Giza. He received his doctorate from Yale University in 1990 with the dissertation "Archaeology of an Image: The Great Sphinx of Giza." Mark Lehner is notable because of his in-depth research on the pharaonic area of Giza, which he has mapped and analyzed. His thorough work led him to discover the pyramid workers' city and to make new discoveries about the pyramids and other monuments of the famous Egyptian plateau.

GREAT SPHINX. From a young age, Lehner was interested in the sphinx because of his interest in the theories of psychic Edgar Cayce. Lehner is one of the Egyptologists who has delved most deeply into the mystery of the sphinx.

From Plundering to Archaeology

The jewels and other luxurious items collected inside the tombs of the pharaohs attracted tomb robbers as early as the time of the Old Kingdom. To prevent grave robbing, in the New Kingdom chambers known as *hypogea* were excavated in the Valley of the Kings. A town was founded near the burial ground— Deir el-Medin—where workers watched over the tombs to protect the peace of the dead kings. Nevertheless, there were cases of workers who allowed the tombs to be robbed in exchange for part of the stolen goods. At the end of the New Kingdom, the tomb robbers, among them a group of priests of Amun, stripped the necropolis at Thebes, leaving the majority of mummies in only their cloth wrappings. Even the mummies were not safe. Bodies were stolen to be ground up and sold as healing powders for superstitious rulers of Europe and Asia.

In the 1800's, hundreds of adventurers collected Egyptian treasure for learned European collectors and museums. The alternative to robbing only came after archaeology took root among the European sciences. In 1835, the Egyptian Antiquities Service was created to protect the treasures and monuments of Ancient Egypt from both domestic and foreign theft.

AUGUSTE MARIETTE
The French archaeologist Auguste Mariette (1821-1881), seated at the photo's center, looks upon items found at an excavation of Saqqara. Mariette was a great defender of the importance of Egyptian treasures.

BELZONI
Depiction of Belzoni dressed in Egyptian clothing.

A European Plunderer

The Italian adventurer Giovanni Battista Belzoni first settled in the United Kingdom, then headed to Alexandria in 1815. Like a bulldozer, he invaded the depths of ancient Egypt, with the support of the British consul. His main targets were Abu Simbel—from which he cleared sand and found the larger temple of Ramses II—and the Valley of the Kings. He shipped the large bust of Ramses II to the British Museum, and also sent the obelisk of Ptolemy IX and the alabaster sarcophagus of Seti I to London.

G. BELZONI.

THE SCHISM OF AKHENATEN
The New Kingdom turned to the worship of Aten, represented by a sun disk. This religion came on the scene for the first time in the Temple of Heliopolis during the rule of Amenhotep II (1426-1400 B.C.). Worship of Aten continued during the reign of Amenhotep III (1390-1353 B.C.). However, it was his successor, Amenhotep IV (1353-1336 B.C.), who proclaimed Aten the only god of Egypt and prohibited the worship of Amun-Re. In the fifth year of his rule, Amenhotep IV changed his name to Akhenaten and founded a new capital, named Akhetaten (Tell el-Amarna). His great royal wife was Nefertiti. After the death of Akhenaten, he, his wife, and the god Aten seem to have

HYPOSTYLE HALL

A *hypostyle* is a roof supported by columns. The pillared hall of the Great Temple of Karnak, with smooth papyrus columns, was built during the rule of Amenhotep III.

been erased from Egyptian memory with one stroke from the moment a nine-year-old boy named Tutankhamun (about 1332-1322 B.C.) became pharaoh. He was the son of Akhenaten, and his royal government was run by the Grand Vizier Ay and Army Commander Horemheb. Centuries later, after his tomb was found nearly intact in 1922, Tutankhamun became the "golden boy" of Ancient Egypt. He continues to be an endless source of surprises and mysteries.

DECADENCE AND INVASIONS

Most notable in the Nineteenth and Twentieth Dynasties is the military Pharaoh Ramses II (about 1279 to 1213 B.C.). This ruler was responsible for the legendary battle against the Hittites (a people who were among the earli-

est inhabitants of what is now Turkey) that was recorded in detail on tablets and which was resolved after signing a peace treaty. This peace treaty was the first in history between two great powers. Ramses II had his accomplishments described triumphantly on the pillars of his funeral temple in Thebes. On the banks of the Nile, he left an extraordinary architectural legacy: two rock-cut temples at Abu Simbel, one dedicated to himself and the other to his wife Nefertari. These were elevated to higher ground in the 1960's when the construction of the Aswan Dam threatened to leave the site underwater.

Ramses II's name in Greek is Ozymandias. Pieces of a statue of Ramses II, found in the desert in the 1800's, inspired the British poet Percy Shelley to write the sonnet *Ozymandias* (1818),

which reflects on time, the passage of power, and the endurance of art.

The new kingdom began to languish after Ramses III (about 1187-1156 B.C.) and ended after the death of Ramses XI.

Pharaonic Egypt continued to decline in the Third Intermediate Period (1075-715 B.C.). Egypt, however, seemed to be reborn when Macedonian Alexander the Great ended Persian rule and was crowned pharaoh (332-331 B.C.). He ruled for scarcely a year, but during that time he founded the city of Alexandria. A brief period of rule by the Macedonian Dynasty was followed by the Ptolemaic Dynasty beginning in 305 B.C. The enigmatic Cleopatra VII was the last queen of Egypt (51-30 B.C.), ruling under the power of imperial Rome.

The Egypt of the Pharaohs

Around 5,000 years ago, on the banks of the Nile, one of the most sophisticated and long-lasting civilizations of ancient times began. Its royal rulers, known as pharaohs, built kingdoms and left one-of-a-kind architectural remains.

The Two Great Capitals

Located in the delta of the Nile, Memphis was the capital of Egypt for a thousand years, until around 2050 B.C. Then, the capital was moved to Thebes, the cradle of the Eleventh Dynasty, which reunified Egypt and founded the Middle Kingdom. Thebes retained its status as capital throughout the entire New Kingdom. And, it may seem strange that lower Egypt is above upper Egypt on the map, but because the Nile flows northward, it makes perfect sense for the land of Egypt.

MAIN SITES

The Nile valley is filled with ruins from ancient Egypt, the fruit of 3,000 years of history. The best-known archaeological sites, in order of antiquity, are the pre-dynastic city of Abydos, site of the Great Temple of Osiris and the oldest royal cemetery in the world; Memphis, with the necropolises of Dahshur, Saqqara, and Giza, which house the pyramids; Thebes, with the temples of Karnak and Luxor, and the Valley of the Kings.

PHARAOHS AND MONUMENTS

① Zoser
(2630-2610 B.C.) Third Dynasty

He built the first stone funeral complex in the world: the Step Pyramid of Saqqara.

② Khufu
(2550-2530 B.C.) Fourth Dynasty

He ordered the Great Pyramid of Giza, his tomb, to be built. He was the father of the Pharaoh Khafra and the grandfather of Menkaure, the other great builders of the pyramids of Giza.

③ Ramses II
(1279-1213 B.C.) Nineteenth Dynasty

Pharaoh, warrior, and builder, he led the famous battle of Kadesh against the Hittite Empire. He built many huge statues, built the temples of Abu Simbel and the Ramesseum, and founded the city of Per-Ramses (Tanis), his capital.

MEDITERRANEAN SEA

Alexandria

Pyramids of Giza

Heliopolis

Giza ②

Saqqara

① Memphis

Step pyramid

Dahshur

LOWER EGYPT

Herakleopolis

Eastern Desert

④ Tell el-Amarna

Amarna Letters

Western Desert

EGYPT

Abydos

Nile River

Deir el-Bahri

Karnak

Valley of the Kings ⑤ Thebes

Enlarged area

⑥

Colossi of Memnon

UPPER EGYPT

N

0   Miles   125

Abu Simbel ③

Why did Thutmose III try to erase the name of his aunt, Hatshepsut, from history?

When Egyptologists discovered that Hatshepsut's name and image had been chiseled off of nearly all of her monuments and temples, Egyptologists first thought it was the revenge of her nephew, Thutmose III. Hatshepsut had started out as co-regent for Thutmose III when her husband and half-brother, Thutmose II, died suddenly. Soon, Hatshepsut was ruling in her own right and only at her death did Thutmose III regain his throne. If Thutmose III was angry at his aunt, however, it makes little sense that he waited to deface her monuments until 20 years after her death. Some Egyptologists now believe that Thutmose III was trying to ensure that his own son, Amenhotep II, ruled after his death, and not a closer relative of Hatshepsut.

❹ Akhenaten
(1353-1336 B.C.) Eighteenth Dynasty

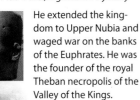

The son of Amenhotep III was the greatest religious reformer of ancient Egypt, enforcing the worship of Aten. He installed his capital at Tell el-Amarna.

Nefertiti
(1353-? B.C.) Eighteenth Dynasty

She was the great royal wife of Akhenaten, who made her co-regent. Some Egyptologists suspect that she inspired the religious schism promoted by her husband.

❺ Thutmose I
(1493-? B.C.) Eighteenth Dynasty

He extended the kingdom to Upper Nubia and waged war on the banks of the Euphrates. He was the founder of the royal Theban necropolis of the Valley of the Kings.

Hatshepsut
(1473-1458 B.C.) Eighteenth Dynasty

Heiress of Thutmose I, she was the most powerful Egyptian queen-pharaoh. She ordered the Temple of Djeser-Djeseru, one of the greatest architectural gems of Ancient Egypt, to be built.

Thutmose III
(1479-1425 B.C.) Eighteenth Dynasty

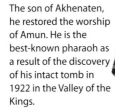

Called "the Great," he was responsible for the greatest territorial expansion of the Egyptian kingdom. He conquered the kingdoms of the Middle East and the Eastern Mediterranean. He built the Temple of Amun-Re at Karnak.

Tutankhamun
(1332-1322 B.C.) Eighteenth Dynasty

The son of Akhenaten, he restored the worship of Amun. He is the best-known pharaoh as a result of the discovery of his intact tomb in 1922 in the Valley of the Kings.

❻ Amenhotep III
(1390-1353 B.C.) Eighteenth Dynasty

His rule was distinguished by the most construction during the time of a single pharaoh in Ancient Egypt. The Colossi of Memnon are the remains of the fabulous temple that was built next to the Nile.

Red Sea

CHRONOLOGY OF ANCIENT EGYPT

Name	Years	Dynasties
Early Period	3100 B.C. –2650 B.C.	I and II
Old Kingdom	2650 B.C. –2150 B.C.	III, IV, V, VI, VII, and VIII
First Intermediate Period	2125 B.C. –1975 B.C.	IX, X and XI
Middle Kingdom	1975 B.C. –1640 B.C.	XI, XII, XII, and XIV
Second Intermediate Period	1630 B.C. –1520 B.C.	XV, XVI, and XVII
New Kingdom	1539 B.C. –1075 B.C.	XVIII, XIX and XX
Third Intermediate Period	1075 B.C. –715 B.C.	XXI, XXII, XXIII, and XXIV
Late Period	715 B.C. –332 B.C.	XXV, XXVI, XXVII, XXVIII, XXIX, XXX and XXXI
Hellenistic Period	332 B.C. –30 B.C.	

THE CENTURIES-OLD CULTURE OF THE NILE

The civilization of ancient Egypt extends approximately from 3200 B.C. to the death of Cleopatra VII in 30 B.C. Conventionally, its history begins with King Narmer, who joined Upper and Lower Egypt and founded the first dynasty. Egyptian history is divided into three high periods—Old Kingdom, Middle Kingdom, and New Kingdom. The height of its splendor was during the Fourth, Eighteenth, and Nineteenth dynasties. The Persian conquest in the 500's B.C. marked the start of the empire's decline.

Symbols of Power

That pharaohs used the same symbols of power for more than 3,000 years highlights the stability and traditional nature of ancient Egyptian society. With few exceptions, the crown, *scepter* (rod or staff carried by a ruler as a symbol of royal power), and other objects that symbolized the power of the pharaoh were used dynasty after dynasty.

Crowns

In ancient Egypt, the crown served a dual political and religious role. That is why the gods are often depicted with a crown, a symbol of their authority over humans. Before the unification of Egypt, the rulers of Lower Egypt were distinguished from those of Upper Egypt by their crowns, each relating to a patron god. The white crown of Upper Egypt (the *hedjet*, at right) was associated with the vulture goddess Nekhbet. The red crown of Lower Egypt (the *desheret*, below) was associated with the snake goddess Wadjet. The combination of the two crowns resulted in the double crown, sometimes called a *pschent*, a symbol of the authority of the pharaoh over the unified "Two Lands." Aside from the royal crown, there were also other crowns for strictly ceremonial or religious use.

KHEPRESH
The blue crown had a religious use, as the pharaohs wore it when making offerings to the gods.

CROWN OF UNITY
The double crown (shown below on the god Horus), or *pschent*, combined the two crowns of Egypt, the *hedjet* and the *desheret*, to make one crown that symbolized a unified Egypt.

SHUTY
Made up of two long feathers, this is the crown of the god Amun. It also symbolizes the union of the Two Lands. In the New Kingdom such crowns were worn by women of the royal house and some priestesses.

DESHERET
This red, cylindrical crown with an upward extending "arm" and a rounded bulge at the front was the crown of Lower Egypt.

HEDJET
The *hedjet* was shaped like an oblong turban and represented the monarchs of Upper Egypt. This was the crown of the Theban dynasties.

Crowns and Materials

One of the most surprising things to archaeologists was the lack of royal crowns in tombs of pharaohs. Some scholars believe that the "Double Crown of the Two Lands" (pictured to the left and on the prior page) became, as in today's monarchies, a precious treasure. It was not buried with a pharaoh, but was instead passed on to the pharaoh's heir and was only used on coronation day (a ceremony at which a king or queen publicly receives a crown as a symbol of rule).

Emblems of Authority

The supreme authority of the pharaoh was not only signified by the crown. Emblems, scepters, diadems, and headdresses were also used as representations of power.

RITUAL BEARD

A false beard was used by the pharaoh on significant occasions. It identified him with the god Osiris, the legendary founder of Egypt.

NEMES

A cloth headdress, the nemes, took the place of the crown during the daily activities of the pharaoh. It was held to the head with a headband.

STAFF AND WHIP

The staff and whip are emblems of royalty. These pastoral instruments designate the pharaoh as leader of his people.

URAEUS

The Uraeus was a representation of Wadjet, the cobra goddess and protector of the pharaohs. Only pharaohs were permitted to wear this symbol on their clothing.

DIADEM

The diadem served to display royal dignity with or without the nemes. They were particularly used, as in the case of the one above, by the sons of the pharaoh.

SEKHEM-SCEPTER

This scepter symbolized strength and the magical power of the pharaoh, the royal family, and the nobility. The image shows Queen Nefertari with the Sekhem-Scepter.

Why Were Pharaohs Mummified?

It was not only the pharaohs who had their bodies *mummified* (carefully preserved after death). By around 5,000 years ago, most wealthy ancient Egyptians arranged to have their bodies mummified after death. Nevertheless, Egypt's most splendid mummies and tombs are those of the pharaohs and royal family, who remain impressive even in death.

Egypt's first mummies were created naturally. They were the result of burying the bodies of the dead in hot, dry, desert sand. These natural mummies began a custom that would last in ancient Egypt for thousands of years. Because of Egyptian religious beliefs, having a corpse that was still recognizable after death had great importance. By about 3500 B.C., the Egyptians were improving upon the natural mummification process. They used *resin* (a sticky yellow or brown substance that flows from certain plants and trees) and linen wrappings to seal the dead body against moisture. The process of mummification in Egypt would become far more elaborate, but this was its beginning.

Why would the Egyptians want to preserve their dead, and especially their dead rulers, so carefully? Why did they go to such trouble?

Egyptians believed that people experienced an *afterlife* (a life after death). They thought the soul lived on, but in order for souls to survive, they needed a body to which they could return after their travels.

As long as the soul could recognize its body, the Egyptians believed all was well for the deceased. So, great care was taken with the treatment of a dead body. Still, the Egyptian people worried that if the body was damaged, the soul would not be able to find its body. The bandaging of a mummy's face sometimes flattened the nose and changed how the face looked, so *embalmers* (people who prepare dead bodies

for burial) often stuffed the nose of the dead to help it keep its shape and keep the face looking right. Sometimes coffins were painted with a likeness of the dead person to make sure that the soul could find its tomb, even if the body had deteriorated. Or, in the case of King Tutankhamun, a likeness was made as a golden mask placed over his face.

In fact, of all the mummies in Egypt, certainly the most elaborate care was taken with the mummies of dead pharaohs. Weapons, jewelry, clothing, furniture, small figurines that were meant to act as servants for the dead pharaoh—all of these items were buried with a pharaoh's mummy to ensure he had everything he needed to be comfortable in the afterlife.

The Opening of the Mouth

Because the ancient Egyptians believed that a dead person's soul needed food and drink to survive in the afterlife, priests at a burial performed a special Opening of the Mouth ritual. They believed this ritual allowed the dead to receive nourishment. The Opening of the Mouth required special tools—including knives and *amulets* (charms often worn around the neck for protection)—and priests chanting spells over the coffin that held the corpse. In this image at left, the mummified King Tutankhamun has this ritual performed for him by Ay, his successor to the throne.

RAMSES II IN DEATH
The wooden coffin case (below
left) and mummy (below right)
of the great pharaoh Ramses II.

Could a Pharaoh's Mummy Come With a Curse?

In 1922, Lord Carnarvon, a British no-bleman, and Howard Carter, a British archaeologist, discovered the tomb of Tutankhamun in the Valley of Kings. When Carnarvon died (probably of blood poisoning) in 1923, people began to talk of curses on those who violated a pharaoh's tomb. For a time after, anyone who had entered Tut's tomb and later died was of great interest to the newspapers. They would report that the "Curse of the Mummy" had claimed another victim. Some tombs did have curses inscribed on them to deter grave robbers. Given that the remains of the dead were deemed necessary for an Egyptian afterlife, and the wealth that was buried with a pharaoh, threats were used to try to keep graves intact. There is no evidence that Tut's tomb carried any written curse upon it. And, the number of deaths that occurred to people involved with this tomb was not greater than would have occurred ordinarily among any group of people—only 6 of the 26 people present when the tomb was opened died within a decade.

Curse from a tomb in Saqqara—"As for anybody who shall enter this tomb in his *impurity* (unclean state): I shall wring his neck as a bird's."

Who Built the First Pyramid?

The Pharaoh Zoser was the first Egyptian ruler to be entombed in a huge stone pyramid. Zoser began a tradition of royal burial in monumental stone pyramids that Egyptian pharaohs continued for more than 1,000 years.

The Pharaoh Zoser (ZOH zur—also spelled Djoser [JOH zur]) ruled Egypt from about 2630 B.C. at the beginning of the Old Kingdom. Zoser and his queen established a strong central government in Egypt. Many great advances in technology, trade, farming, and architecture were made during their reign. The nation grew in wealth and power as many new cities rose along the banks of the Nile River.

Like pharaohs before him, Zoser began planning a magnificent tomb long before his death. Ancient Egyptians had long-established funeral customs designed to ease a pharaoh into the afterlife. Since as early as the Predynastic Period (before around 3100 B.C.), rulers had been buried beneath a massive low platform with sloping sides, called a *mastaba*. Mastabas were constructed of mud bricks. Underneath a mastaba, a pharaoh might be buried within a network of tunnels and chambers that were designed to protect the tomb and its contents from robbers.

Zoser called upon his trusted *vizier* (advisor) Imhotep—a noted architect, priest, physician, and statesman—to build his tomb. Imhotep began by constructing a large mastaba for Zoser in the ancient Egyptian city of Memphis. He made important innovations, however, that would forever change the way pharaohs built their tombs.

Firstly, Imhotep used cutstone blocks instead of mud bricks to build the mastaba. From this time forward, Egyptian pharaohs built their tombs from stone.

Secondly, what started out as a single mastaba became something very different as Imhotep aimed to build a tomb suitable for a great pharaoh. Imhotep built another mastaba on top of the first, and then another on top of the second, and so on. Eventually, Zoser's tomb

rose up about 200 feet (60 meters), in a series of six giant platforms (or steps), one on top of another. Each platform was slightly smaller than the one below it, forming the familiar four-sided, pointed shape of a pyramid. At the time this pyramid, the first step pyramid, was built, it was the largest stone monument in the world.

A complicated series of deep tunnels and chambers in Zoser's pyramid created a sort of underground palace for the pharaoh and his family to enjoy in the afterlife. Some chambers served as chapels. Others were used to store treasures and other items the pharaoh would need in the afterlife.

Unfortunately, the remains of Zoser and the treasures that filled his tomb are lost. Long ago, tomb robbers broke into the underground chambers and carried off the contents. However, Zoser's pyramid still stands today in the Egyptian village of Saqqarah, near present-day Cairo.

PYRAMID OF ZOSER

Many scholars believe that the pyramid shape had a special religious meaning to the Egyptians. The sloping sides may have reminded the Egyptians of the slanting rays of the sun, by which the soul of the king could climb to the sky and join the gods.

Imhotep

Scholars recognize Zoser's step pyramid as the first pyramid built in ancient Egypt. They believe that Imhotep (above), the architect of this magnificent monument, also invented many of the tools that were used for pyramid construction. After his death, the Egyptians worshipped Imhotep as a god for his many contributions to Egyptian civilization.

Building a Pyramid

The ancient Egyptians had no machinery or iron tools to build the pyramids. They cut huge limestone blocks from nearby quarries with simple copper chisels and saws. Gangs of men dragged the blocks to the pyramid site and pushed the first layer of stones into place to form a large platform. Then they built long ramps of earth and brick and dragged the stones up the ramps to form the next layer. As they finished each layer, they raised and lengthened the ramps.

Inside the Great Pyramid

A cross section of the Great Pyramid in Egypt shows the Grand Gallery, the King's Chamber, the Queen's Chamber, and various passages. After the burial, large blocks called sealing plugs were allowed to slide down the passageway from the Grand Gallery to seal off the tomb. Workers left the tomb through an escape passageway.

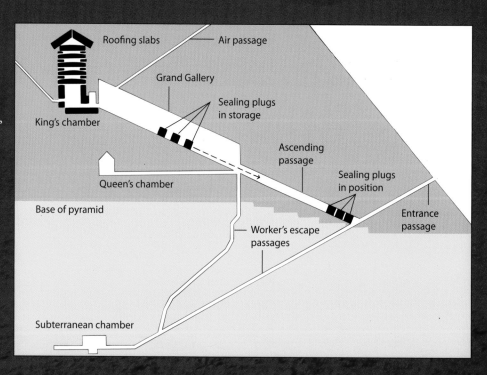

Roofing slabs

Air passage

Grand Gallery

Sealing plugs in storage

King's chamber

Ascending passage

Sealing plugs in position

Queen's chamber

Entrance passage

Base of pyramid

Worker's escape passages

Subterranean chamber

Which Pharaoh Built the Greatest of the Pyramids?

The Great Pyramid of Giza was built by Pharaoh Khufu in the 2500's B.C. It was originally 481 feet (147 meters) tall, but some of its upper stones are gone now and it stands about 450 feet (140 meters) high. It was 3,500 years before a building taller than the Great Pyramid was built; in the A.D.1200's and 1300's, cathedrals in England finally began to top this pyramid's height.

The Egyptians thought a pharaoh needed a preserved body for an afterlife. But pyramids were not truly necessary to the afterlife of a pharaoh. A large burial chamber could easily have been carved underground to protect a tomb and provide a luxurious afterlife without building a huge structure above. The pyramids were mostly a way for a pharaoh to display how wealthy and important he was (or believed he was).

When Khufu (shown in the statue at left) came to the throne as a young man in his 20's, he immediately began planning his pyramid tomb.

People once believed his Great Pyramid (the center pyramid in the photo above) was built by slaves. Today, however, experts think that Egyptian citizens were "drafted"—that is, men were asked by the government to give a certain amount of time each year to pyramid work. The Great Pyramid probably took more than 20 years to build.

If Khufu built the Great Pyramid to be remembered in the future, it was a success. We are remembering him right now some 4,500 years after his death. If, however, he hoped the pyramid would provide a suitable place for his mummified body, then he was not so successful. Khufu's mummy has never been found, and the burial chamber of his pyramid is empty.

Near the Great Pyramid, there are temples, tombs, and two smaller pyramids built by Khufu's son Khafre and grandson Menkaure. There is also the magnificent Great Sphinx, likely built by Khafre.

The Great Sphinx of Giza

To the east of the pyramid of Khafre stands the Great Sphinx, the greatest and oldest of all statues. This *colossal* (huge) figure of a lion with a human head fascinates visitors today as it did more than 4,000 years ago when it was created.

Sentinel and Protector

The Sphinx was carved in limestone from the quarry of the Great Pyramid. Its construction is attributed to Khafre. The head, supposedly a portrait of Khafre, was carved into a hard layer of rock, while the body was sculpted in softer stone and thus has eroded more. For centuries, the colossal figure was covered by desert sand, and over the course of history it has been repaired using mud bricks, stones, and cement. It was created as a lookout figure, part of Khafre's funerary complex, and it was a *sentinel* (guard) and protector of the sacred grounds of Giza.

Dimensions

Construction date:
Between 2600-2500 B.C.

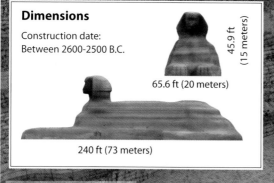

45.9 ft (15 meters)

65.6 ft (20 meters)

240 ft (73 meters)

Stele

The *stele* (an upright slab or pillar of stone bearing an inscription) of Thutmose IV, or the Dream Stele, is slab of granite 7 ft (2.1 m) tall, weighing several tons. It is partially damaged.

Missing Nose

Arab chronicles of the A.D. 1400's report that the face of the Great Sphinx was defaced at that time by Mamluks (a mainly Turkish-speaking military group that ruled Egypt from about A.D. 1250 to 1517).

(Almost) Lost in the Sands of Time

Sand has often buried the Great Sphinx up to its neck. King Thutmose IV of Egypt (who ruled about 1400 to 1390 B.C.) cleared the sand away, supposedly after dreaming that the god Horus asked him to do so. During modern times, workers removed the sand in 1818, 1886, 1926, and 1938.

Color
Experts believe that during the time of the Old Kingdom the body and face were painted red.

Headdress
The nemes (Egyptian headdress) was painted in horizontal stripes of yellow and blue.

Location
The Sphinx lies in a deep pit, near the east end of the causeway leading to the pyramid of Khafre.
Egyptologists suggest that, given its unusual location with respect to the central axis of the Pyramid of Khafre and the Temple of the Sphinx, the carving of the Sphinx was not planned out in detail, but rather improvised after finding a suitable rock.

Great Sphinx

0   N   655 ft

GIZA NECROPOLIS

1 Pyramid of Khufu
2 Pyramid of Khafre
3 Funerary Temple of Khafre
4 Valley Temple of Khafre
5 Temple of the Sphinx
6 Pyramid of Menkaure
7 Tomb of Queen Khentkawes
8 Valley Temple of Menkaure
9 Pyramids of the Queens
10 Tomb of Heminu

The Beard of the Sphinx
Among the restoration projects of the ancient glories of Egypt undertaken by the kings of the Eighteenth Dynasty was the Great Sphinx. Not only did they place the first protective layers of masonry, they also adorned it with the braided beard of the deities. However, it fell off before long.

The Sphinx as seen by Western artists

1615	1681	1755	1798	1838	1858	1887	1925
George Sandys	Cornelis de Bruijn	Frederic Norden	Vivant Denon	David Roberts	Francis Frith	Henri Béchard	Émile Baraize

Did They Marry Their Sisters?

Some pharaohs from the New Kingdom (1539-1075 B.C.) did marry their sisters, and less often their daughters, in order to keep the supreme power within their family line.

The pharaoh was considered god on Earth, the reincarnation of Osiris. It was Osiris who conquered death with the help of his sister-wife Isis. Osiris and Isis had a child together, Horus. Imitating the founding gods of Egypt, their heirs on Earth—the pharaohs—married their blood relations.

Overall, marriages between closely related members of the royal family were an infrequent practice, confined to particular times in Ancient Egypt, essentially to the New Kingdom and the Ptolemaic period (around 300 to 30 B.C.).

Succession to the throne was established in such a way that the women of the royal family held the rights to the throne. Thus, an heir to the throne had to marry one of the daughters of the great royal wife of his father. In this way they maintained the sacred character of the pharaoh's family line, the source of their absolute power.

During the Second Intermediate Period (1630-1520 B.C.), Ahhotep I married her eldest brother Seqenenre Tao. Their son, Ahmose I, who threw out the Hyksos and founded the Eighteenth Dynasty (1539-1292 B.C.) of the New Kingdom, followed the example of his parents and also married several of his sisters. One of them, Ahmose-Nefertari, became his "Great Royal Wife and Mistress of The Two Lands" and was promoted to "God's Wife." This was a title passed from mother to daughter that recognized a woman's royal origin, purity of their blood, and the legitimacy of ancestry.

Ahmose and Ahmose-Nefertari gave birth to Amenhotep I, who also married his sister Ahmose-Meritamon and did not leave male heirs. To legitimatize himself as a pharaoh, his successor, Thutmose I, commander of the Egyptian army, had to take the daughter (or sister) of his predecessor as his wife.

The Pharaoh-Queen Hatshepsut, daughter of Thutmose I, also had to maintain the tradition and marry her half-brother, Thutmose II.

FATHERS AND DAUGHTERS

While marriage between brothers and sisters was the more common form of close family marriage, there were also marriages between fathers and daughters, though much less frequently.

Outside of the Egyptian royal court, Egyptian society considered sibling marriage and marriages between other close relatives unacceptable.

DIVINE MODEL

The *triad* (set of three) formed by the sibling gods of Osiris (in the middle), Isis (to the right) and their son Horus, was the family model of the rulers of ancient Egypt.

AMENHOTEP I AND AHMOSE-MERITAMON

Marriage between Siblings

Problems due to *consanguinity* (KON sang GWIHN uh tee, a close blood relationship) became obvious during the reign of Amenhotep I. None of his offspring reached adult age.

RAMSES II AND BINTANATH

Marriage between Father and Daughter

Meritamon, Bintanath, and Nebettawy were all great royal wives of their father. Henuttawy, another daughter, was a secondary wife. Ramses II had children with most of these wives.

Akhenaten and Nefertiti

The Pharaoh Akhenaten and his wife, the beautiful Nefertiti, have gone down in history as a couple in love. Together they led a religious revolution, and then the queen suddenly disappeared without a trace.

Akhenaten and Nefertiti were one of the most famous couples of ancient Egypt. However, the story of the king and his beloved wife is full of mysteries.

Akhenaten was born Amenhotep, and he was the second son of Amenhotep II and his great royal wife, Tiye. Raised by his mother, who was not from the royal line but was the daughter of a high nobleman of the court of Thutmose IV, young Amenhotep was introduced to the worship of Aten, a new god with great importance within the royal family.

Once Amenhotep was pharaoh, as Amenhotep IV, he sought to promote the worship of this new god and to reduce the power that was held by the priests of Amun, the most popular of the Egyptian gods in the New Kingdom. Amun was credited with aiding the Egyptians in driving out the Hyksos. Due to the gifts of the faithful, the priests of Amun had become wealthy and powerful enough to pose a threat to the pharaoh, and were even capable of interfering in the royal succession.

To avoid this, during the fifth year of his rule, Amenhotep IV began a religious revolution. He imposed the worship of Aten (represented by the sun disk) and changed his name to Akhenaten (meaning *the one who benefits Aten*). He proclaimed himself high priest of Aten, the only person able to communicate between men and the new supreme god. Furthermore, emphasizing the *schism* (SIHZ uhm—division or split), he left Thebes and founded a new city further north. He called the city Akhetaten (meaning *the horizon of Aten*) and moved the royal court there. This location is now called Tell el-Amarna. Akhenaten also started a new artistic style, a more natural and familiar way of showing the royal family.

His Great Royal Wife was Nefertiti *(the beautiful has arrived),* who may be the best-known Egyptian queen because of the famous bust of her on display in Berlin. Nefertiti played an important role in establishing the new religion, such that the schism was blamed on her. Judging by the archaeological findings, her political and religious importance was extraordinary. She was given the name Neferneferuaten *(the most perfect of Aten's perfections).* She was even depicted in art with a club in hand striking enemies—an image usually reserved for pharaohs—and in ceremonial scenes on an equal footing with her husband. She also

Did Akhenaten Have a Genetic Disease?

Because of the unusual way in which Akhenaten appears in art—with enlarged breasts and hips, and elongated facial features—various genetic conditions have been attributed to him. Because of his elongated features and long limbs, some experts have speculated he may have had Marfan Syndrome, a disorder affecting the body's connective tissues. Other experts have thought Akhenaten may have had a genetic disease that caused him to appear more female than other men. DNA testing on his mummy could answer this question. A mummy that is a relative of Tutankhamun's was found in the 2000's, but it is not certain that the mummy is Akhenaten.

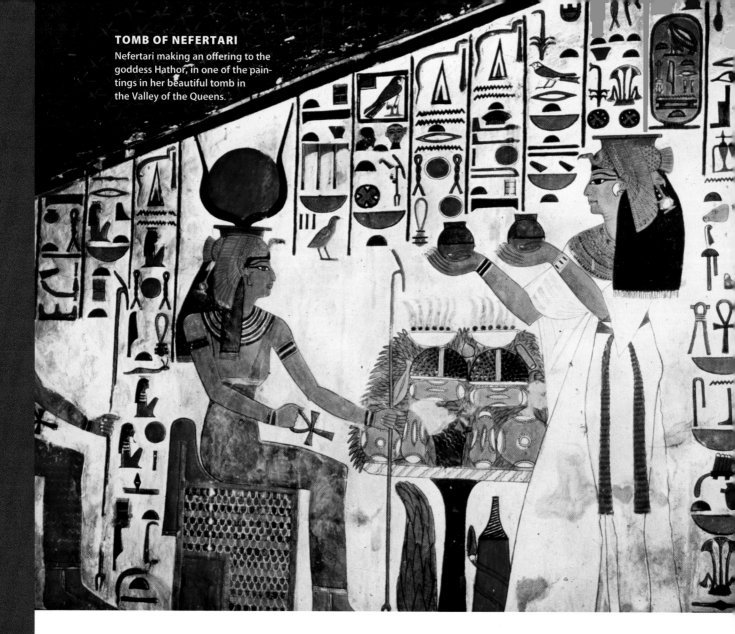

TOMB OF NEFERTARI
Nefertari making an offering to the goddess Hathor, in one of the paintings in her beautiful tomb in the Valley of the Queens.

had temples exclusively for the worship of Aten, such as Hut-Benben.

MYSTERIOUS NEFERTITI

Unlike the pharaoh, Nefertiti's origins are obscure. Some authors believe that she was a Mitanni princess. Others believe that she was the daughter of Ay, brother of Tiye, Akhenaten's mother. Either way, based on the images passed down to us, her marriage to the pharaoh—with whom she had six daughters—was a happy one, at least until the 12th year of his reign.

From that year onward, the prominence of Nefertiti wanes and records of her soon completely disappear. A painful event, likely the death of Meketaten, the second of the daughters of the royal couple, may have preceded this rapid eclipse. Shortly after that tragic event came the death of Tiye, Akhenaten's beloved mother.

DISAPPEARANCE AND DISCOVERIES

Confronted with the sudden disappearance of the queen, Egyptologists hold several theories among

them. The first and simplest is that Nefertiti died the following year. That would be why the king married his and his wife's oldest daughter, Meritaten. The second is that, fallen from grace for some unknown reason, she was cast off by her husband. Perhaps, embarrassed by misfortune, Akhenaten attributed the death of his daughter to a punishment from Aten for the lack of male heirs, which the pharaoh blamed on his wife. Others, however, believe that Nefertiti kept close to her husband. Archaeological findings

regarding the confusing last years of Akhenaten seem to indicate that Nefertiti in fact died and that the regency sometimes attributed to her actually corresponded to Meritaten.

The lack of references to Nefertiti in the last years of the pharaoh's reign has intrigued generations of Egyptologists, who do not rule out the possibility that the revenge of the priests of Amun extended to the queen's remains, and condemned her to the worst punishment imaginable: erasing her name from history.

QUEEN TIYE
Bust of Tiye, wife of
Amenhotep III and
mother of Akhenaten.

Women of Power

When we think of the queens of ancient Egypt, after the beautiful Nefertiti and the doomed Cleopatra (see pages 38-39), we are often unable to name any others. But Egypt had a number of important and powerful queens. Some of them ruled with political power in their own right, and others exerted power from behind the scenes, using their influence with the pharaoh who was a son or husband to effect change.

Hatshepsut, as discussed previously, was the first type of monarch, ruling in her own right. Her 20-year reign as a pharaoh was a time of great prosperity for Egypt; she greatly increased trade with neighboring nations. Not until Cleopatra ruled some 1,400 years later would a woman again wield the full power of an Egyptian pharaoh.

Tiye, Great Royal Wife of Amenhotep III and mother of Akhenaten, was the latter sort of queen. She was a trusted advisor to both her husband and son and was an important influence at both of their courts. While living with her at her court as a boy, Akhenaten was introduced to the religion of the one god Aten.

Nefertari, Great Royal Wife of Ramses II, was also powerful through the king to whom she was married. Her importance to Ramses II is shown in the honors he accorded her. In addition to having the most lavish tomb in the Valley of Queens at Luxor, Ramses II built a temple dedicated to her at Abu Simbel that stood next to his own temple.

Artistic Ideals

In 1912, in the workshop of the sculptor Thutmose in Tell-el-Amarna, the German archaeologist Ludwig Borchardt discovered the famous multicolored bust of Nefertiti. Comparison with the faces of other Egyptian sculptures led some Egyptologists to believe that the face of the beautiful Nefertiti was being represented in an ideal form and not necessarily as she had truly looked. A study using computed tomography may have confirmed this by discovering a face inside the sculpture that is refined, but with different facial features. It is possible the bust was started by the artist for another woman, and then the commission was changed to a request for the bust of Nefertiti. Or, it is possible that the bust of Nefertiti portrays the artistic ideals of the Amarna period (the period during the reign of Akhenaten), rather than reality.

Decline and Recovery

The strength of the Egyptian society of the New Kingdom is evident. Half a century after Akhenaten's religious revolution, Egypt recovered its prestige thanks to Seti I, who reconquered the territories that were lost in the Middle East during the confused and troubled reign of Akhenaten.

Akhenaten's Capital

The campaign against *monotheism* (worship of a single god) begun in ancient Egypt by Akhenaten must have been fierce, judging by the few remains of Akhetaten (Tell el-Amarna, in image left). The capital built by Akhenaten was taken apart and condemned to oblivion by the powerful priests of Amun. Akhetaten virtually disappeared into the desert sands.

INSCRIPTIONS Hieroglyphic inscriptions recorded in stone in the magnificent palace of Seti I at Abydos.

Who Were the Black Pharaohs?

Ancient Egypt's decline accelerated rapidly after about 1075 B.C. During the next 750 years, 10 foreign dynasties ruled Egypt as conquerors. Between about 750 and 660 B.C., the Nubian rulers of Kush, a kingdom to the south, conquered Egypt. The Nubian rulers of this period are sometimes called the "black pharaohs."

The ancient Egyptians had diplomatic and trade relationships with other peoples in Africa and beyond. The ancient Egyptians spoke a language that was related both to the Semitic languages of southwestern Asia and to certain languages of northern Africa. They had a complex economic and political relationship with Nubia, an ancient state to the south. Like Egypt, Nubia extended along the Nile River. It reached from the southern boundary of ancient Egypt south to present-day Khartoum, Sudan.

Egypt occasionally invaded and controlled Nubia. At other times, the Nubians were allies and some served in the pharaoh's army. The tomb of Mesehti, a high-ranking Egyptian official of the Middle Kingdom, contained 40 painted wooden statuettes representing a group of dark-skinned Nubian archers.

Powerful independent states that rivaled Egypt also emerged in Nubia. The earliest of these states was Kerma. The kingdom of Kerma lasted from about 2400 to 1500 B.C. Another kingdom, called Kush, developed in Nubia after 1000 B.C. Kush grew into a wealthy and powerful center of agriculture and trade just as Egypt was weakened by rulers fighting among themselves. Around 750 B.C., a Kush king named Piye invaded and conquered Egypt. He proclaimed himself a true pharaoh of Egypt and founded the Twenty-fifth Dynasty, known as the Kushite and based in the city of Thebes.

Piye did not wish to govern over Egypt, so he retreated back to Nubia, leaving Egypt without effective rulers. When he died in 716 B.C., he was buried in an Egyptian-style pyramid tomb at el-Kurru in Nubia. His brother Shabaka then invaded Egypt and crowned himself pharaoh. His reign was followed by the Pharaohs Shebitku and Taharqa. These Kushite rulers are today often known as the "black pharaohs" due to their Nubian ancestry. They revived the tradition of burial in pyramid tombs that had not been used since the Old Kingdom. The tradition of pyramid tombs then continued for hundreds of years in Nubia.

The reign of the black pharaohs ended with Taharqa around 664 B.C., when the Assyrians invaded and conquered Egypt from the north. The Kushite rulers were pushed back into Nubia. There, they reigned over a powerful kingdom for centuries. But the Kushites never invaded or conquered Egypt again.

NUBIAN ARCHERS
Small wooden models were placed in tombs to magically perform the work of living servants—the statues to the right were archers to guard the pharaoh.

Different Peoples Depicted in Ancient Egyptian Art

Scholars know the ancient Egyptians considered themselves a distinct people compared to neighboring peoples and foreigners. The Egyptians distinguished themselves from Nubian, Libyan, Semitic, Berber, and Eurasian peoples that they met and traded with throughout the Egyptian empire. The Egyptians saw themselves as darker skinned than peoples they called Asiatics and Libyans. They saw themselves as lighter skinned compared to the Nubian peoples to the south. They also observed differences in hair, facial features, and even body build compared to other peoples.

During the Old Kingdom, artistic traditions determined how people were shown in statues, reliefs, and paintings. People were not necessarily portrayed as they looked in life. Egyptian men were depicted with reddish brown skin, while women were shown with a yellowish white skin tone.

By the Middle Kingdom and in the New Kingdom people were depicted in art in a more realistic manner. Distinctive facial features are more apparent in art from these periods. Many portraits of people of ancient Egypt are known from tombs and caskets that held their mummies. In most Egyptian tombs, the owners are depicted with brown complexions. Foreigners in this period are depicted realistically in hair style, facial features, and complexion.

PEOPLE OF DIFFERENT LANDS
Egyptian artists depicted people from Nubia and people from the Near East differently from each other and themselves.

Who Was Cleopatra?

Cleopatra VII was an heir of the Ptolemaic Greek Dynasty and a symbol of Egyptian culture. She was Ancient Egypt's last hope for recovering their influence in a world dominated by Roman rule.

She was born into the ruling dynasty of the Ptolemy family, started by Ptolemy I in 323 B.C. Ptolemy was born in Macedonia, a region north of Greece. Ptolemy became a leading general in the army of Alexander the Great (356-323 B.C.), a Macedonian king who built an empire that included Egypt and most of western Asia. After Alexander died in 323 B.C., Ptolemy gained control of Egypt. The Macedonians were culturally Greek and Greek speaking.

Daughter of Ptolemy XII Neos Dionysos and his sister Cleopatra V Tryphaena, Cleopatra VII, at age 14, was appointed to rule along with her father and her brother Ptolemy XIII, who was 10. Upon the death of her father in 51 B.C., she married her brother, as was the custom, to reaffirm her power as pharaoh and win public favor. This she gained quickly, as she was the first of her family line to speak Egyptian; her ancestors had kept their Greek culture and language.

The alleged beauty of the young Queen Cleopatra aroused the desire of the two most powerful men of the age, the Roman generals Julius Caesar and Mark Antony. With Julius Caesar she had a son, Ptolemy VI, also known as Caesarion. After Julius Caesar's assassination, she married Mark Antony and gave birth to twins. However, despite her romantic bond with these generals, Cleopatra aimed to preserve the independence of Egypt and defied the power of Rome, represented in the form of Octavian, Mark Antony's rival.

THE LAST QUEEN

In his *Life of Antony*, the Greek historian and biographer Plutarch (A.D. 46-119) described Cleopatra as a woman of conventional beauty, but as possessing great powers of speech, capable of dazzling her listeners with the persuasion of her words. The death of Cleopatra, which took place during the year 30 B.C., ended 3,000 years of pharaonic Egyptian history. Defeat in the naval battle of Actium (31 B.C.) left Egypt open for Octavian to annex it to Rome. To avoid the humiliation of defeat, Mark Antony killed himself. Tradition has it that Cleopatra let herself be bitten by an asp. It is also possible that she was killed by poison that she took on Octavian's orders.

Mystery

Not even Plutarch, the first to write of the death of Cleopatra, had the courage to confirm that the last queen of Egypt had died as he described. After saying that she had committed suicide and that an asp had injected her with its poison, he added that there were other opinions about how it had been administered, such as through a hollow knife, and concluded: "That is how they say it happened." In reality, how it happened is not known. Historians do not rule out the idea that Cleopatra was murdered and that Octavian spread a story designed to beautify her death and calm her supporters. Even though the specifics remain unresolved, experts agree that poison was the fatal agent.

Where Is Cleopatra's Tomb?

Queen Cleopatra's body has never been discovered. A team of archaeologists thought that the mystery was solved in 2008 when they identified the area of Taposiris Magna, a site 30 miles (48 kilometers) west of Alexandria, as the place of her burial, alongside the tombstone of Mark Antony. However, no body has been discovered.

CLEOPATRA
A Roman coin with a profile of the queen.

Identification of Mummies

Establishing the identity of a person who died thousands of years ago requires using several disciplines and combining information from historical texts, archaeological findings, *anthropology* (the scientific study of humanity and of human culture), and technological advances in medicine.

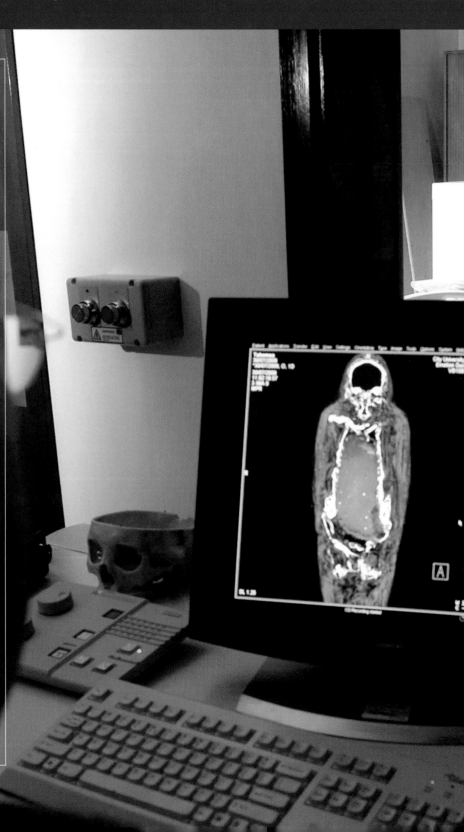

X rays

The use of X rays as tool to assist with the identification of mummies became less critical once computed tomography, with its advanced features, was invented. Nevertheless, X ray is still a common initial technique, and it is especially useful in locating skeletal malformations that can identify a person.

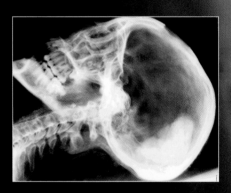

DENTAL AGE DETERMINATION

The X ray of the skull (top) and the mummy of the "Young Lady," found in tomb KV35, which British Egyptologist Joann Fletcher wrongly attributed to Nefertiti in 2003. The skull image plates serve to determine the person's age by the teeth and cranial joints. In this case, it was found that the "Young Lady," the mother of Tutankhamen, was about 25 years old when she died.

Archaeological Support

The lists of the kings of ancient Egypt that have been discovered—for example, the royal lists of Karnak and Abydos, shown in the image to the left—are essential references for the identification of mummies.

DNA Revelations

DNA identification tests have revolutionized the world of Egyptology. Not only have they uncovered the identity of unknown mummies, as was the case with Queen Tiye, but they also confirmed the practice of royal intermarriage during the Eighteenth Dynasty. Thanks to DNA testing, it has been discovered that the mother of Tutankhamen was one of Akhenaten's five sisters.

1 NO CONTAMINATION After selecting the mummy to be researched, scientists take protective measures to avoid contaminating it with traces of their own DNA.

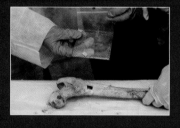

2 TAKING SAMPLES Samples are taken from different parts of the mummy's body, especially the inside of the bones. This area is useful because it is most protected from outside contamination.

3 ANALYSIS In the laboratory, the genetic makeup of the tissue sample is analyzed. The mummy's gender is established.

4 MATCHES DNA is compared and matches in DNA are looked for.

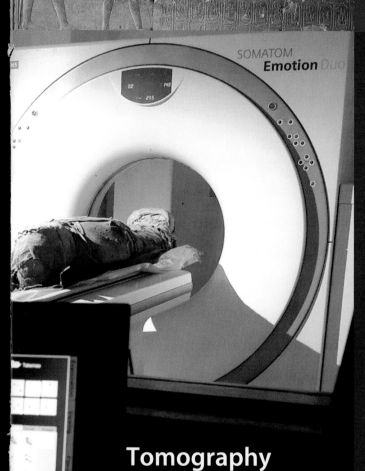

Tomography

Computed tomography is very valuable to Egyptologists because it allows for the analysis of mummified bodies without cutting open a mummy. This imaging system, which provides three-dimensional high-resolution images, can detect unusual traits with high accuracy. This helps with identification of a mummy.

Places to See and Visit

OTHER PLACES OF INTEREST

THE GIZA SPHINX AND PYRAMID
CAIRO, EGYPT

The Great Sphinx and Great Pyramid of Giza are impressive and beautiful.

MIT RAHINA
EGYPT

In this small town, visitors can see the ruins of Memphis, the capital of ancient Egypt. An open-air museum has been set up here, allowing visitors to walk among the remains that give hints of the city's former splendor. Highlights include monumental statues, sphinxes, and archaeological remnants of palaces and temples.

MONUMENTS BY RAMSES II
ABU SIMBEL, EGYPT

Cut from the rocks in southern Egypt, on the west bank of Lake Nasser, they form part of the Open Air Museum of Nubia and Aswan. These colossal twin temples were built around 1274 B.C. and are dedicated to the worship of Ramses II and his wife Nefertari. They are some of Egypt's best-preserved monuments.

UNIVERSITY OF PENNSYLVANIA MUSEUM OF ARCHAEOLOGY AND ANTHROPOLOGY
PHILADELPHIA

The collection of over 42,000 objects of Egyptian art is considered one of the best in the world. Among its treasures is an enormous granite sphinx of Ramses II from around 1200 B.C.

ARCHAEOLOGICAL MUSEUM
FLORENCE, ITALY

This museum houses an exhibition of more than 14,000 pieces.

Memphis

SAQQARA

This is the site of one of the largest necropolises in Egypt and the most important in the ancient capital of Memphis. It was used for more than 3,000 years. Various funerary monuments are found here, including 17 pyramids for pharaohs, royal tombs in subterranean chambers, and mausoleums for dignitaries and nobles.

ZOSER FUNERARY COMPLEX

Visitors can access this complex in Saqqara, which includes the well known Step Pyramid of Zoser, constructed by Imhotep, the first architect known to history. The complex also contains the remains of various temples, chapels, trenches, and a system of passageways where stone coffins have been found.

SERAPEUM

The bulls of Apis were the most sacred animals in Egypt. This underground necropolis, where the bulls were buried in stone coffins after embalming (treatment with spices, chemicals, or drugs to prevent decay), is found to the north of Saqqara.

Amarna

Akhenaten stripped Thebes of its status as the capital city and raised a new city midway between Thebes and Memphis in the 1300's B.C.. The city carried the name of Akhetaten, the "Horizon of Aten," and was built quickly. And as quickly as it bloomed, it was destroyed. Today some of its ruins, such as the unfinished tomb of the heretic pharaoh, can be visited.

METROPOLITAN MUSEUM OF ART

NEW YORK CITY

This museum has a large collection of Egyptian art exhibited in 40 galleries encompassing more than 26,000 objects running from Paleolithic to Roman times. Many of these objects were found through excavations performed by the Museum between 1906 and 1941.

OBELISKS

LONDON, NEW YORK CITY, PARIS, ROME

Of standing obelisks, there are 27 outside of Egypt and 6 remaining in Egypt. Some of the best-known outside of Egypt include the Lateran Obelisk in Rome in the Piazza di san Giovanni. The Romans were enchanted with Egyptian obelisks, and they brought 13 of them to Rome. Three other cities each have obelisks named "Cleopatra's Needle," although the obelisks predate Cleopatra VII by centuries. London's Cleopatra's Needle is at the Victoria Embankment on the bank of the Thames. The needle in New York City is in Central Park, just west of the Metropolitan Museum of Art. Obelisks were always made in pairs. and the London and New York obelisks are twins. The Parisian obelisk is in the Place de la Concorde. Its twin is in Luxor.

Glossary

Afterlife— Life after death.

Amulet— Charms often worn around the neck for protection.

Anthropology— The scientific study of humanity and of human culture.

Archaeology— The scientific study of the remains of past human cultures.

Civilization— A society or culture that has complex social, political, and economic institutions.

Computed tomography— Or CT, an advanced type of X ray.

Consanguinity— A close blood relationship.

Coronation— A ceremony at which a king or queen publicly receives a crown as a symbol of rule.

Cuneiform— An ancient writing system that used wedge-shaped letters.

Delta— A low plain composed of sediments deposited at the mouth of a river.

DNA—Chainlike molecules found in every living cell on earth that direct the formation, growth, and reproduction of cells and organisms.

Dynasty— A series of rulers who belong to the same family.

Embalm— To treat a dead body with spices, chemicals, or drugs to prevent decay.

Embalmer— A person who prepares dead bodies for burial or entombment.

Egyptologist— Scientists who study ancient Egypt.

Genetics— The scientific study of heredity, the passing on of characteristics of living organisms from one generation to the next.

Hypogeum— (plural, hypogea) An underground burial chamber.

Incantation— Words spoken or chanted as a magic charm or to cast a magic spell.

Inscription— Letters or symbols carved in such substances as clay or stone.

Legends— Stories from the past.

Metempsychosis— The movement of the soul from one body to another at death.

Monotheism— Worship of a single god.

Mummified— A body that has been carefully preserved through natural or artificial means.

Myth— A story of unknown origin, often one that attempts to account for events in nature or historical events from long ago.

Nomad— A person who moves from place to place as a way of obtaining food.

Oasis— A fertile area in a desert where underground water comes close enough to the surface for wells.

Obelisk— Great, upright, four-sided stone pillars.

Relief— Figures or designs that project from a surface in sculpture or carving.

Rituals— Religious ceremonies.

Scepter— Rod or staff carried by a ruler as a symbol of royal power.

Schism— Division or split.

Scribes— People who write and copy texts for a living.

Sentinel—Guard.

Smelting— Obtaining metal from ore by melting it.

Stele—An upright slab or pillar of stone bearing an inscription.

Vizier— Advisor.

For Further Information

Books

Hyde, Natalie. *King Tut*. New York: Crabtree, 2014. Print.

Maitland, Margaret. *Pharaoh: King of Egypt*. London: British Museum, 2012. Print.

Quirke, Stephen. *Who Were the Pharaohs?* London: British Museum, 2010. Print.

Shaw, Garry J. *The Pharaoh: Life at Court and on Campaign*. London: Thames & Hudson, 2012. Print.

Tyldesley, Joyce A. *The Pharaohs*. London: Quercus, 2009. Print.

Websites

Clark, Liesl, and Peter Tyson. "Explore Ancient Egypt." *Nova*. PBS, 23 June 2011. Web. 03 Mar. 2014.

"Egyptians." *BBC History*. BBC, 2014. Web. 03 Mar. 2014.

"Life in Ancient Egypt." *Carnegie Museum of Natural History*. Carnegie Museum of Natural History, n.d. Web. 03 Mar. 2014.

"List of Rulers of Ancient Egypt and Nubia." *Heilbrunn Timeline of Art History*. The Metropolitan Museum of Art, 2013. Web. 03 Mar. 2014.

"Pharaoh: King of Egypt." *British Museum*. Trustees of the British Museum, n.d. Web. 03 Mar. 2014.

Index

A

Abu Simbel, Temples of, 9, 12, 14-
    16, 33, 42
Abydos, 11, 16, 34-35, 41
Afterlife, 10, 20-22, 25
Aha, 8-10
Ahhotep I, 28
Ahmose I, 11, 28
Ahmose-Meritamon, 28, 29
Ahmose-Nefertari, 28
Akhenaten, 7, 14-15, 17, 41, 43;
    genetic disease question, 31;
    marriage, 30-33; reaction
    against, 14-15, 34-35
Akhetaten, 14, 30, 34-35, 43
Alexander the Great, 15, 38
Alexandria, 14, 15
Amarna Age, 7, 33, 43
Amenhotep I, 28, 29
Amenhotep II, 14, 30
Amenhotep III, 14, 15, 17, 33
Amenhotep IV. See Akhenaten
Amun, 14, 18, 30, 32, 35
Amun-Re, 12, 14, 17
Antony, Mark, 38, 39
Archaeological Museum
    (Florence), 42
Archaeology, 6, 14
Aten, 7, 14-15, 30, 33, 43
Avaris, 11
Ay, 15, 32

B

Baraise, Émile, 27
Beards, 6, 19, 27
Béchard, Henri, 27
Belzoni, Giovanni Battista, 14
Bintanath, 29
Borchardt, Ludwig, 33
Bruijn, Cornelis de, 27
Bulls of Apis, 43

C

Caesar, Julius, 38
Carnarvon, Lord, 21
Carter, Howard, 21
Cayce, Edgar, 6-7, 13
Cleopatra VII, 15, 17, 33, 38-39, 43
Cleopatra's Needles, 43

Computed tomography, 13, 33,
    40-41
Crowns, 18-19
Cuneiform, 8

D

Denon, Vivant, 27
Desheret, 18
Desroches-Noblecourt, Christiane,
    12
Diadems, 19
DNA studies, 7, 31, 41
Dream Stele, 26
Dreyer, Gunter, 8
Dynasty Zero, 8

E

Early Dynastic Period, 8, 10, 17
Egypt, Ancient, 6-7; history, 8-15;
    map and timeline, 16-17;
    Nubian conquest, 36-37; people
    depicted in art, 37; places to
    visit, 42-43
Egyptologists, 8, 12-14, 27, 33

F

First Intermediate Period, 10, 17
Fletcher, Joann, 40
Frith, Francis, 27

G

Giza, 6-7, 10, 13, 16, 27. See also
    Great Pyramid; Great Sphinx
Grave robbers, 12, 14, 22
Great Pyramid, 6, 10, 13, 16, 24-26,
    42
Great Sphinx, 6-7, 10, 13, 25-27, 42

H

Hatshepsut, 6-7, 12, 13, 17, 28, 33;
    Temple of, 10, 11
Hawass, Zahi, 13
Hedjet, 18
Heliopolis, 11, 14
Henuttawy, 29
Herakleopolis, 10, 16
Herodotus, 8
Histories (Herodotus), 8
Hittites, 15
Horus, 8, 18, 28, 29

Hyksos, 11, 28, 30
Hypogea, 12, 14
Hypostyle Hall, 14-15

I

Imhotep, 22-23, 43
Isis, 28, 29

K

Karnak, 41; Temple of, 11, 12, 14-15
Kerma, 36
Khafre, 10, 25-27
Khepresh, 18
Khufu, 6, 10, 16, 24-25, 27
Kush, 36

L

Lehner, Mark, 6-7, 13
Lower Egypt, 8, 10, 16, 18

M

Macedonia, 15, 38
Marfan syndrome, 31
Mariette, Auguste, 14
Martin, Geoffrey T., 12
Mastabas, 22
Meketaten, 32
Memphis, 10, 16, 22, 42, 43
Menes, 8-10
Menkaure, 10, 25, 27
Mentuhotep, 10
Meritamon, 29
Meritaten, 32
Mesehti, 36
Metropolitan Museum of Art, 43
Middle Kingdom, 10-11, 16, 17,
    36, 37
Mit Rahina, 42
Mummies, 31, 37; curse, 21; grave
    robbing, 14; identification
    methods, 40-41; Khufu, 25;
    mummification process, 20;
    Tutankhamun, 20, 21
Museum of Archaeology and
    Anthropology (Philadelphia),
    42

N

Narmer, 8-10
Nebettawy, 29

Necropoleis, 10, 14, 27, 43
Nefertari, 15, 19, 33, 42
Nefertiti, 7, 14-15, 17, 30-32, 40; bust
    of, 30, 33
Nemes, 19
New Kingdom, 11-17, 28, 30, 34, 37
Nile River, 8, 11, 15, 16, 22, 36
Nomads, 8
Norden, Frederic, 27
Nubia, 8, 11, 12, 36-37

O

Obelisks, 11, 43
Octavian, 38, 39
Old Kingdom, 10, 14, 17, 22, 36, 37
Opening of the Mouth ritual, 20
Osiris, 16, 28, 29
Ozymandias (Shelley), 15

P

Pharaohs, 6-7; beginnings, 8-10; black,
    36-37; blood-relation marriages,
    7, 28-29; mummification, 20-21;
    places to visit, 42-43; symbols of
    power, 18-19. See also by name
Piye, 36
Plutarch, 38, 39
Predynastic Period, 8, 22
Ptolemy I, 38
Ptolemy XIII, 38
Pyramid Texts, 10
Pyramids: construction, 23; Geza
    necropolis, 27; last, 11; New
    Kingdom, 11-12; Nubian, 36; of
    Khufu, 6, 10, 16, 24-25, 27; Old
    Kingdom, 10-11; step, of Zoser,
    10, 16, 22-23, 43. See also Great
    Pyramid

R

Ramses II, 9, 14-16, 29, 33, 42;
    mummy, 21
Reeves, Nicholas, 12
Rhomboid Pyramid, 10
Roberts, David, 27
Rome, Ancient, 15, 38

S

Sandys, George, 27
Saqqara, 10, 16, 21, 22, 43

Scepters, 18, 19
Schism of Akhenaten, 14-15, 30
Scorpion I, 8
Second Intermediate Period, 17, 28
Senusret, 11
Seqenenre Tao, 28
Serapeum, 43
Seti I, 34-35
Shabaka, 36
Shebitku, 36
Shelley, Percy B., 15
Shuty, 18
Snefru, 10
Sphinx, Great. See Great Sphinx

T

Taharqa, 36
Thebes, 12, 15, 30, 36, 43; as capital, 10,
    11, 16
Third Intermediate Period, 15, 17
Thutmose (sculptor), 33
Thutmose I, 12, 17, 28
Thutmose II, 28
Thutmose III, 7, 12, 17
Thutmose IV, 30
Tiye, 13, 32, 33, 41
Tutankhamun, 15, 17, 40, 41; mummy,
    7, 13, 20, 21

U

Umm el-Qaab, 8
Upper Egypt, 8, 16, 18
Uraeus, 19

V

Valley of the Kings, 12-14, 16
Valley of the Queens, 32, 33

W

Women: as rulers, 6-7, 33; blood-
    relation marriages, 28-29

X

X rays, 40

Y

"Young Lady" mummy, 40

Z

Zoser, 10-11, 16, 22-23, 43

Acknowledgments

Pictures:

© ACL

© Age Fotostock

© Alamy Images

© Album

© Egyptian National Museum/Bridgeman Art Library

© Corbis/Cordon Press

© Cordon Press

© Getty Images

© Nicholas Reeves

© Shutterstock

© Album/Prisma/SuperStock

© Thinkstock